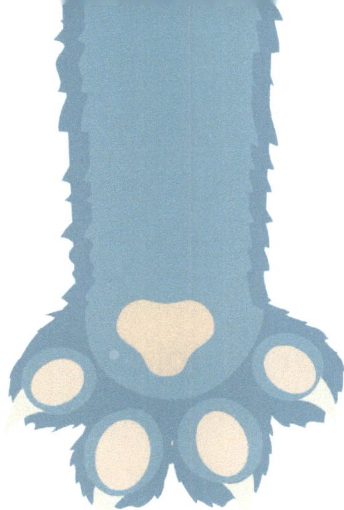

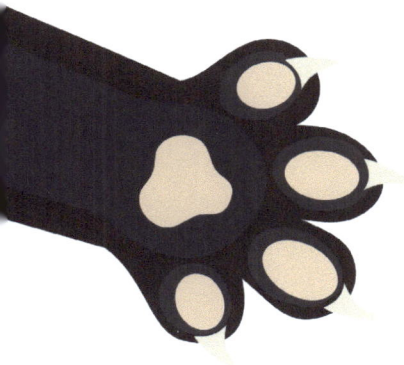

ISBN: 979-8-9904026-0-7

Scan for your free
Cutie Says No - Feelings & Boundaries
Worksheet Package

ACKNOWLEDGEMENT

A big thanks to our cats, Boots and Sammy, for entering our lives and weaving this real-life story.

Another big thanks to our cat, Sunshine, for learning valuable cat skills as a kitten from Boots and being a great dad to our four kittens who entered his life just when he became an adult. It was fun watching him teach the kittens hunting skills that he himself learnt from Boots, and help Sammy out, grooming the kittens and maintaining crowd control.

I am also grateful for our kittens: Cutie, Paws, Fuzzy and Sprinter for being in our lives and adding so much joy and love.

A big thanks to Robert Immings for his invaluable help with graphics, formatting, and everything else that helped to make this book a reality.

My heartfelt gratitude to Dr. Ashley Owen, Behavioral Medicine Director, Emory Family Medicine Residency Program, and Ms. Bindu Bakka, M.I.T, Elementary and Middle School teacher, for their reviews that helped shape the final version of the book.

Last but not the least, I owe a big thanks to my family:

..to my son for his excitement and support with the creation of this book

..to my father for being a role model as a poet

..to my mom for instilling the love of reading and literature in me and for leading the way in making learning fun at every age.

And most importantly, a big thank you to you, my dear reader, for choosing this book. I hope it fills your days with as much fun and joy as our cats bring to our lives.

There once was a kitten named
Cutie:

With pretty spots, she was a
Beauty!

She was so very nice, a real
Sweetie!

But one day, her li'l brother
Fuzzy

Kept biting li'l Cutie like
Crazy!

Fuzzy was teething so
Badly

He felt he'd to bite Cutie,
Sadly!

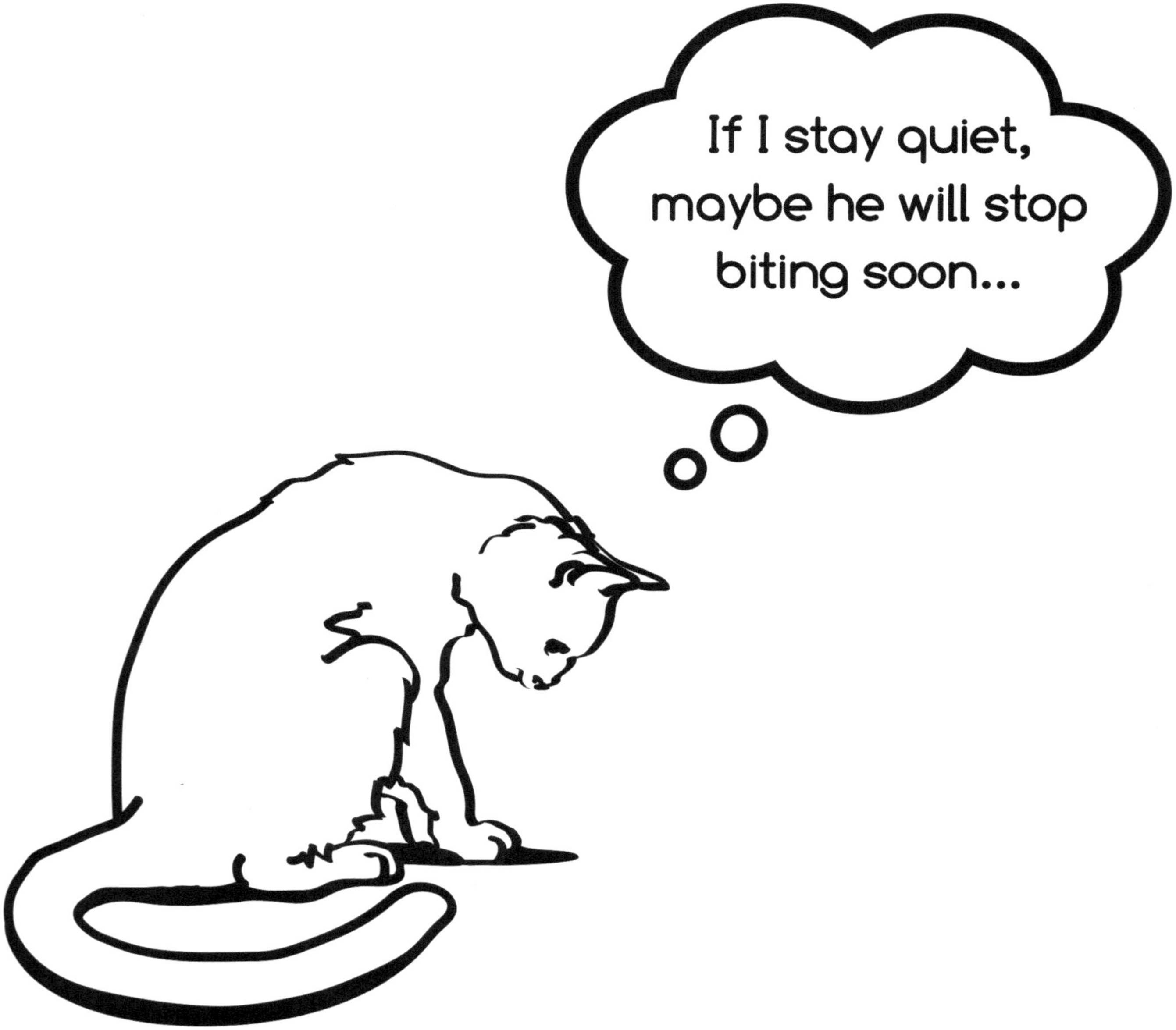
If I stay quiet, maybe he will stop biting soon...

But Cutie felt bad to tell
Fuzzy --

The bites didn't feel so
Cozy,

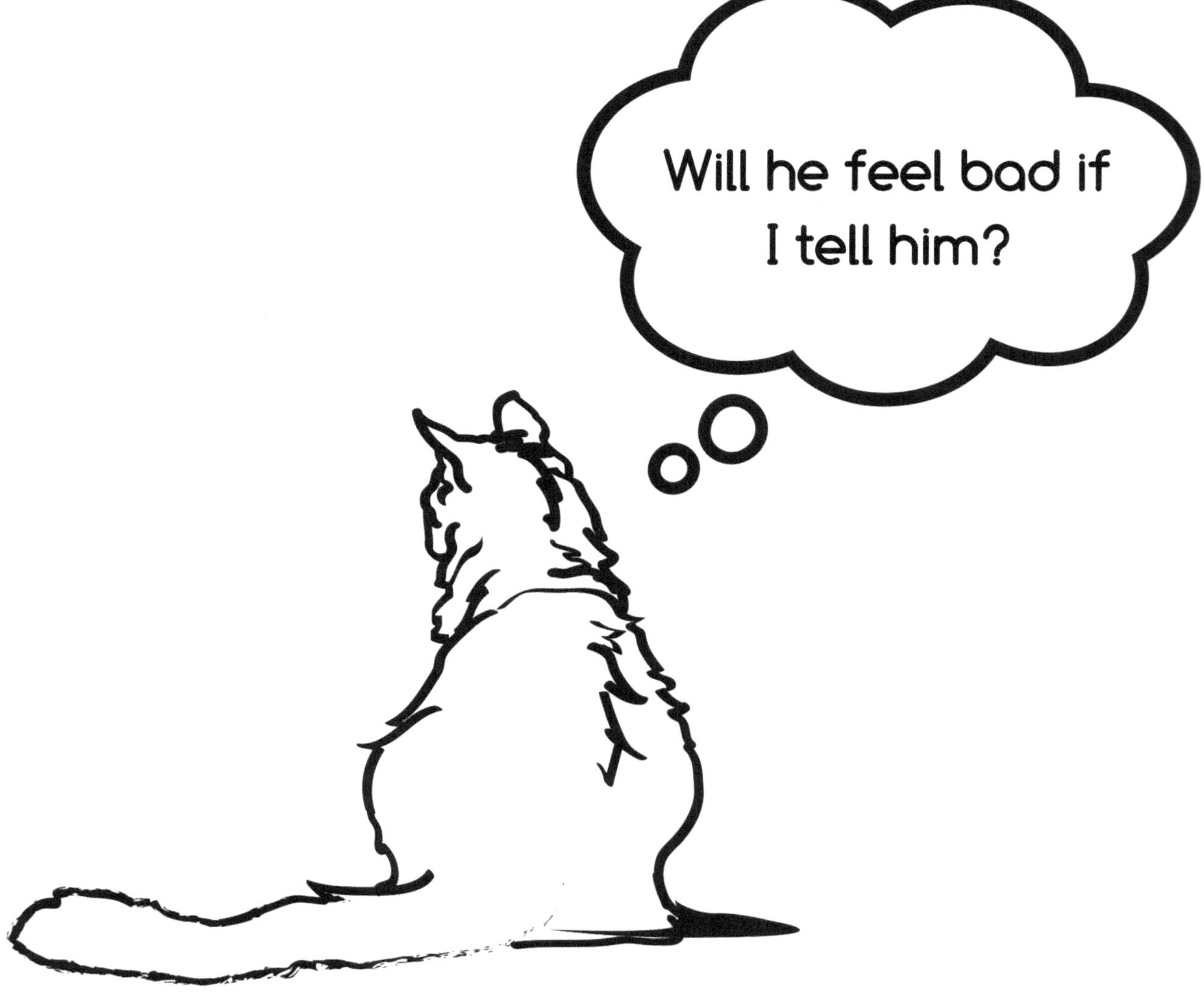
Will he feel bad if
I tell him?

She felt she would upset her
Brother

To tell him the bites were a
Bother

So she felt all the pain but didn't
Say it,

And let him bite till she couldn't
Take it.

Her mom, Sammy, saw Cutie's
Sad eyes,

And helped Cutie find her
Voice.

"It's ok to share how you're
Feeling

So he doesn't hurt you when he's
Teething."

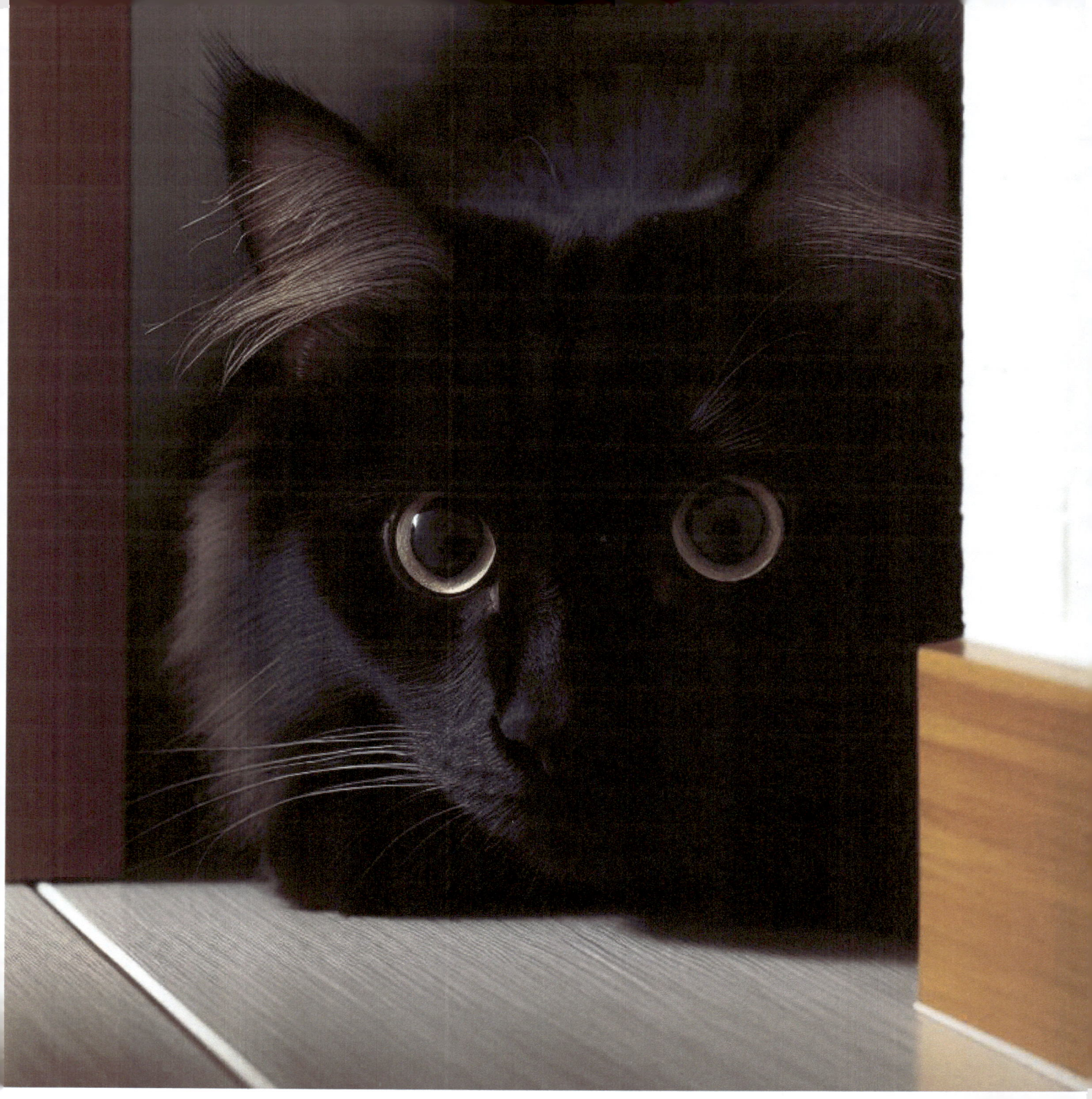

"I tried moving far so he'd
Not bite,

But he followed me and bit the
Same site.

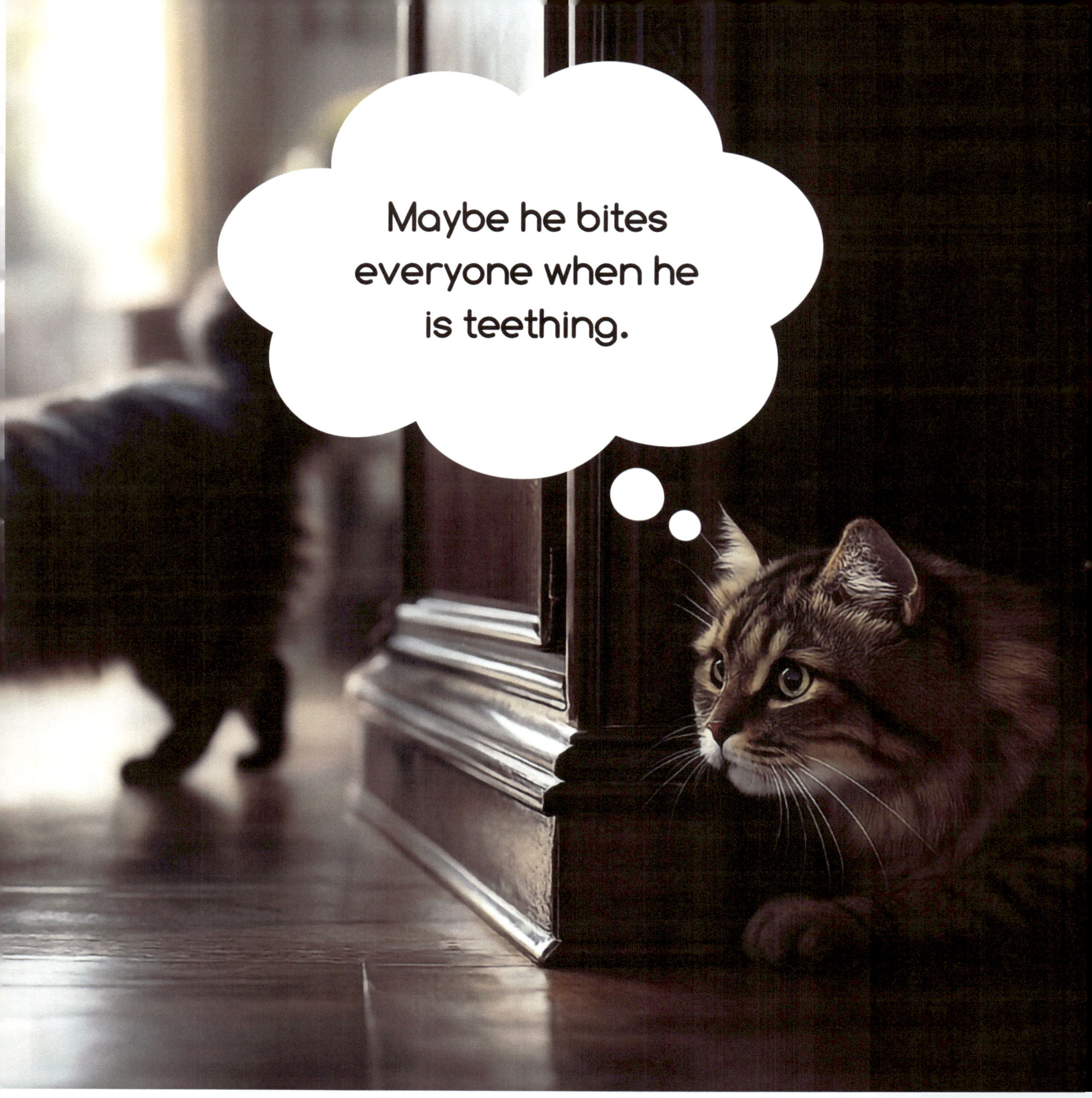
Maybe he bites everyone when he is teething.

So I felt bad to say it was
Hurting,

I felt he'd to bite when he's
Teething,"

"If I say no to dear
Fuzzy,

Will he think I'm being
Fussy?"

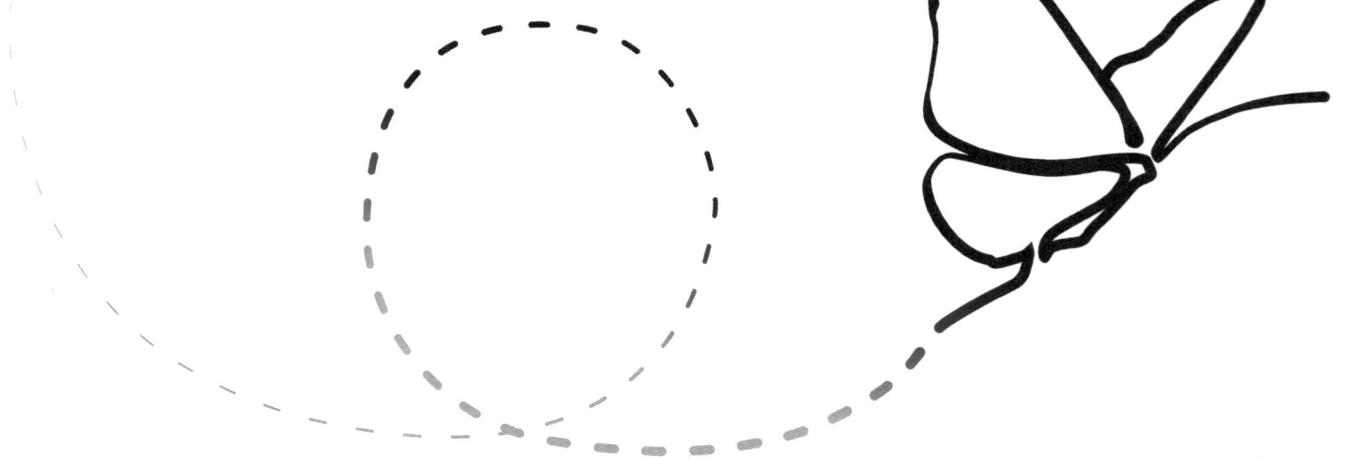

And whispering softly to
Sammy,

"Will he still want to play
With me?"

Cutie told Sammy so
Frankly.

Sammy hugged Cutie so
Tightly,

And said, "Cutie, I see your
Thinking,

But Fuzzy doesn't know he shouldn't be
Biting.

It's ok to tell him it's
Hurting

When he bites you, though he is
Teething.

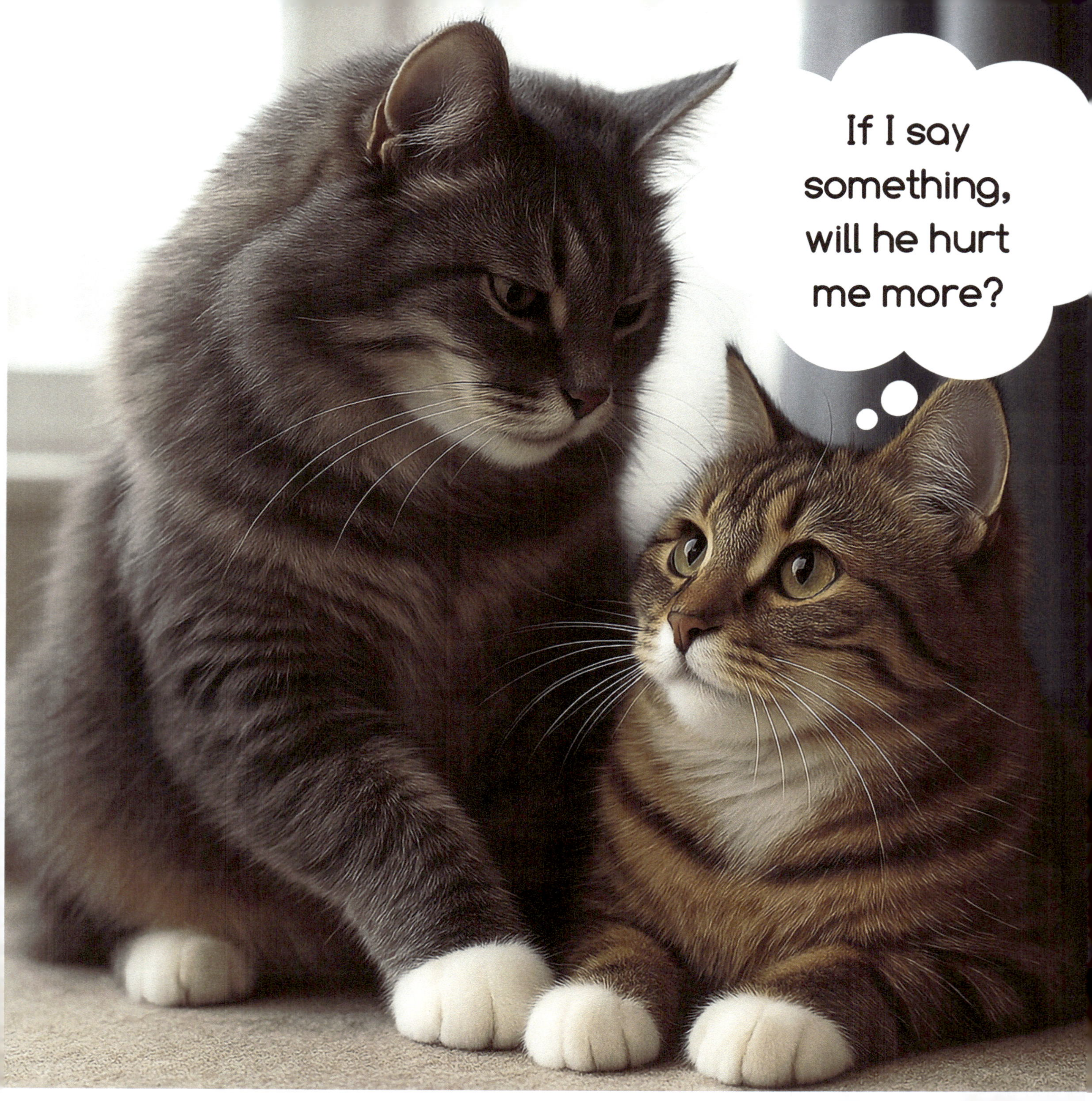
If I say something, will he hurt me more?

I'll keep you safe, I will be
With you

As you say it's not ok to
Bite you."

Cutie felt happy to
Hear this!

She was glad her mom knew how to
Fix this.

The next time that Fuzzy pounced
On her

And sank his teeth into her
Pretty fur,

Cutie got up and said,
"Fuzzy,

It's really not ok to
Bite me!

For when you bite, it hurts so
Badly,

It so hurts my feelings too,
Sadly."

Fuzzy was shocked to hear Cutie!

"I'm so sorry my dear Sissy!

Didn't know I was hurting you,
Truly!"

Fuzzy stopped biting li'l
Cutie.

Cutie was glad she told
Fuzzy

How his bites hurt her so
Deeply.

Now she was spared all the
Biting

From Fuzzy going through the
Teething.

Sammy was proud of li'l
Cutie

For sharing her feelings with
Fuzzy.

If someone should try to
Hurt you

It is ok for you to say
No, too!

Scan for your free

Cutie Says No - Feelings & Boundaries Worksheet Package

www.ingramcontent.com/pod-product-compliance
Lightning Source LLC
Chambersburg PA
CBHW060813090426
42737CB00002B/53